MAJESTIC HORSES

THOROUGHBREDS

by Pamela Dell

Published in the United States of America by The Child's World®
PO Box 326 • Chanhassen, MN 55317-0326
800-599-READ • www.childsworld.com

PHOTO CREDITS
© Bettmann/Corbis: 15
© Corbis: 7
© Eliot J. Schechter/epa/Corbis: 21
© Hulton-Deutsch Collection/Corbis: 16
© Juan Jose Gutierrez Barrow/BigStockPhoto.com: cover, 1
© Juniors Bildarchiv/Alamy: 26
© Kevin R. Morris/Corbis: 12, 22
© Kit Houghton/Corbis: 8
© Mark Abraham/epa/Corbis: 4
© Mark J. Barrett/Alamy: 19
© M. Timothy O'Keefe/Alamy: 11
© Tim Graham/Tim Graham Photo Library/Corbis: 25

ACKNOWLEDGMENTS
The Child's World®: Mary Berendes, Publishing Director;
Katherine Stevenson, Editor

Content Adviser: Weezee

The Design Lab: Kathleen Petelinsek, Design and Page Production

LIBRARY OF CONGRESS CATALOGING-IN-PUBLICATION DATA
Dell, Pamela.
  Thoroughbreds / by Pamela Dell.
    p. cm. — (Majestic horses)
  Includes bibliographical references and index.
  ISBN 1-59296-786-8 (library bound : alk. paper)
  1. Thoroughbred horse—Juvenile literature. I. Title. II. Series.
  SF293.T5D43 2007
  636.1'32—dc22   2006022649

TABLE OF CONTENTS

★ BORN TO RACE!

A loud bell clangs. The starting gates slam open. Powerful horses spring from the gates. The horses thunder down the track. The race is on!

This is the life of the Thoroughbred. These horses are born ready to race. They love to run. In the world of racing, few other **breeds** compare. The drive to race—and win—is in the Thoroughbred's blood.

Training and racing Thoroughbreds costs a lot of money. Some Thoroughbreds sell for millions of dollars. Winning a big race can bring in lots of money, too.

◄ Thoroughbreds work hard when they run! Riders try to make it easier for them to go fast. They crouch down and pull their legs in tight.

Thoroughbreds are proud, beautiful horses. They stand tall. They look at the world with widely spaced, bright eyes. People cannot help but look back!

Everything about a Thoroughbred is long and smooth. Its head sits high, and its neck is well curved. Its powerful body moves easily. Its long legs are made for a fast, even **gallop**. Thoroughbreds can run a long way without getting tired. Their big lungs help them take in lots of air. Some horses can pull heavier loads or carry more weight. But none can run like a Thoroughbred!

Thoroughbreds are fast! They can run as fast as 40 miles (64 kilometers) an hour. That is almost 60 feet (18 meters) every second!

This Thoroughbred is galloping on a farm in England. ▶

8

A Thoroughbred's long back legs act like springs. They help the horse run fast.

A horse's height is measured at the **withers**. Thoroughbreds are 60 to 68 inches (152 to 173 centimeters) tall. People also use the word "hands" to say how tall a horse is. A hand is 4 inches (10 centimeters). Most Thoroughbreds stand 15 to 17 hands high. They weigh about 1,000 to 1,300 pounds (450 to 590 kilograms).

Thoroughbreds' coats are a solid color. They are almost always **bay**, brown, **chestnut**, or black. Sometimes they are gray. Many Thoroughbreds have white markings on their faces or legs.

◀ This bay Thoroughbred lives on a farm in England. You can see his brown color and black mane and tail.

Even before they are born, Thoroughbreds get attention. Owners choose which **stallions** and **mares** will have babies. They want the **foals** to grow into fast, strong horses.

Most newborn Thoroughbreds weigh about 110 pounds (50 kilograms). A newborn Thoroughbred has long legs! It can stand soon after it is born. The foal drinks its mother's milk and grows quickly. Foals gain about 2 pounds (1 kilogram) a day.

This mare and her foal live on a Florida horse farm. ▶

All Thoroughbreds born in the same year are given the same "birthday." In the northern half of the world, their birthday is January 1. On the next January 1, all of these foals become "yearlings." Even a foal born in December would become a yearling on January 1.

In the southern half of the world, Thoroughbreds have a different "birthday." Their birthday is August 1.

Why is this done? Because it makes things easier when the horses start racing. The young horses can race against others with the same birthday. That way they are racing against horses of about the same age.

◀ These three yearlings live on a farm in Kentucky.

Thoroughbreds go back some 300 years. They came from a mix of English horses and other horses.

People have always enjoyed horse racing. By the late 1600s, many people in England loved the sport. English horses were strong and could run a long way. But racing fans wanted faster horses. So they brought some from other countries. Many of these new horses were fast, beautiful Arabians. The newcomers had babies with English horses. The owners kept choosing which horses would have babies. They kept trying to make stronger, faster animals. These horses became Thoroughbreds.

Horse racing is sometimes called "The Sport of Kings." England's King Charles II was a great rider who loved racing. He and other wealthy people brought lots of horses to England.

This drawing of a horse race is from 1665. ▶

ENGRAVED BY C. HUNT

Today's Thoroughbreds came from three stallions—the Byerly Turk, the Godolphin Barb, and the Darley Arabian. These stallions were brought to England in the late 1600s and early 1700s.

Soon Americans wanted Thoroughbreds, too. People brought English Thoroughbreds to North America in the 1700s. The first American Thoroughbred race took place in 1745.

People in England started keeping track of Thoroughbred families in the 1700s. They wrote down which stallions and mares had babies. In America, people started keeping track in the 1800s. Those records are still kept today. Owners know the names of their Thoroughbreds' parents, grandparents, and great-grandparents. They can trace their horses' families back to when the breed began.

◄ This drawing is from 1852. It shows people and Thoroughbreds before a race in England.

WHAT ARE THOROUGHBREDS LIKE?

Many Thoroughbreds tend to be high-strung. That means they get upset or nervous easily. If something surprises them, they might shy away or rear up. They need gentle, careful handling. They are quieter around people they trust.

Thoroughbreds are smart. They also want to win. When they are racing, they give it everything they have. People love their spirit and bravery!

Racing is hard work. People expect a lot out of racehorses. Once Thoroughbreds stop racing, they often get calmer.

The photographer's camera made this Thoroughbred nervous. The horse ran and kicked until the photographer went away. ▶

19

Today, horse racing is one of the sports people enjoy most. It is also a big money-making business. Millions of people go to racetracks every year. The best Thoroughbreds win lots of money for their owners. Every owner dreams of a big win!

It takes lots of hard work and training to be a winner. Only the very best Thoroughbreds get that far. When the horses are yearlings, they start learning how to race. They learn to let a **jockey** ride them. They learn to run around a track. They learn to start from a starting gate. And they exercise to grow strong.

In Thoroughbred racing, jockeys are small and light. Most of them weigh less than 105 pounds (48 kilograms). They are strong, and they are excellent riders.

These Thoroughbreds have just finished a race called the Breeder's Cup. When a race is over, jockeys stand up a little. This helps the horses to slow down. ▶

Another kind of horse racing is called the *steeplechase*. The horses must jump over things like fences and hedges.

Most Thoroughbreds start racing when they are two years old. There are special races for two-year-olds and for three-year-olds. And there are special races for males and females—**colts** and **fillies**.

Racing is hard on a horse's legs and body. Some Thoroughbreds stop racing when they are still young. Some do their best racing when they are three or four. And some keep racing until they are about ten.

What happens to winners after they stop racing? Their owners hope these horses will have lots of foals. They hope the foals will be even faster than the parents!

◄ The mare in this picture no longer races. Instead, she lives on a Kentucky horse farm. One of the foals in this picture is hers. The other foal belongs to another mare.

Not every Thoroughbred is a winner. Some Thoroughbreds never race at all. But there are lots of other things Thoroughbreds can do. Often, they need different kinds of training.

In horse shows, some of the most beautiful animals are Thoroughbreds. Thoroughbreds can also be great jumpers. People use them for other kinds of riding, too. Many people use them for playing polo. And they can make wonderful riding horses and family pets.

Polo is played by two teams on horseback. The riders use long sticks to hit a ball. They try to hit the ball through the other team's goalposts.

Polo horses must run fast and turn quickly. Polo can be a dangerous game! Riders must be skilled and know their horses well. ▶

★ ★ ★ THOROUGHBREDS TODAY

The best-known American races are the Kentucky Derby, the Preakness, and the Belmont Stakes. These races are for three-year-olds. Only eleven horses have won all three races—the "Triple Crown."

Wherever people love racing, you will find Thoroughbreds! The United States has the largest number of Thoroughbreds. It has the biggest racing business, too. England still has lots of Thoroughbreds. So do many other countries. In fact, people own and race Thoroughbreds all over the world.

Why do so many people love these horses? They are exciting animals. They are beautiful even when they are standing still. And when they run, they are like nothing else!

◀ This Thoroughbred is resting in a meadow in England.

★ ★ ★ BODY PARTS
OF A HORSE

1. Ears
2. Forelock
3. Forehead
4. Eyes
5. Nostril
6. Lips
7. Muzzle
8. Chin
9. Cheek
10. Neck
11. Shoulder
12. Chest
13. Forearm
14. Knee
15. Cannon
16. Coronet
17. Hoof

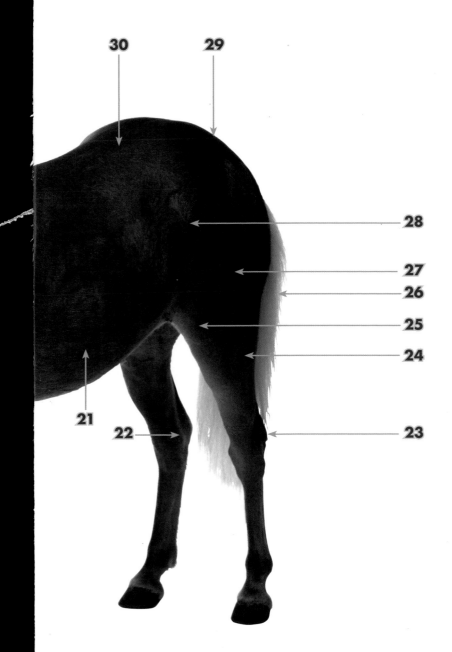

18. Pastern
19. Fetlock
20. Elbow
21. Barrel
22. Chestnut
23. Hock
24. Gaskin
25. Stifle
26. Tail
27. Thigh
28. Point of hip
29. Croup
30. Loin
31. Back
32. Withers
33. Mane
34. Poll

GLOSSARY

bay (BAY) A bay horse is brown with a black mane and tail. Many Thoroughbreds are bays.

breeds (BREEDZ) Breeds are certain types of an animal. Thoroughbreds are a well-known horse breed.

chestnut (CHEST-nut) A chestnut horse is reddish brown with a brown mane and tail. Many Thoroughbreds are chestnuts.

colts (KOHLTZ) Colts are young male horses. When Thoroughbred colts turn five, they are called stallions.

fillies (FIH-leez) Fillies are young female horses. When Thoroughbred fillies turn five, they are called mares.

foals (FOHLZ) Foals are baby horses. Some Thoroughbred foals sell for millions of dollars.

gallop (GA-lup) When horses gallop, they run fast. Thoroughbreds gallop smoothly and quickly.

jockey (JAH-kee) A jockey is a person who rides horses in races. Jockeys in Thoroughbred racing are small and strong.

mares (MAIRZ) Mares are female horses. People choose which Thoroughbred mares will have babies.

stallions (STAL-yunz) Stallions are male horses. All modern Thoroughbreds came from three long-ago stallions in England.

withers (WIH-thurz) The withers is the highest part of a horse's back. A Thoroughbred's height is measured at the withers.

TO FIND OUT MORE

In the Library

Baker, Kent. *Thoroughbred Racing*. Philadelphia, PA: Chelsea House, 2002.

Driscoll, Laura. *Horses*. New York: Grosset & Dunlap, 1997.

Hartley Edwards, Elwyn. *Horses*. New York: Dorling Kindersley, 1993.

Stone, Lynn M. *Thoroughbreds*. Vero Beach, FL: Rourke, 1998.

On the Web

Visit our Web site for lots of links about Thoroughbred horses:
http://www.childsworld.com/links

Note to Parents, Teachers, and Librarians: We routinely check our Web links
to make sure they're safe, active sites—so encourage your readers to check them out!

INDEX

About the author: Pamela Dell is the author of more than fifty books for young people. She likes writing about four-legged animals as well as insects, birds, famous people, and interesting times in history. She has published both fiction and nonfiction books and has also created several interactive computer games for kids. Pamela divides her time between Los Angeles, where the weather is mostly warm and sunny all year, and Chicago, where she loves how wildly the seasons change every few months.